Concrete Is More Beautiful Disfigured and Stained

Also by Snežana Žabić

The Breath Capital (New Meridian Arts)
Broken Records (punctum books)
Po(jest)zija/Po(eat)ry, co-written with Ivana Percl (SKC NS)
U jednom životu (KOS)

Concrete Is More Beautiful Disfigured and Stained

poems

Snežana Žabić

Chicago | Los Angeles

Concrete Is More Beautiful Disfigured and Stained

Published in the United States by Match Factory Editions, 2025

ISBN 978-1-966253-03-7 (hardcover)
ISBN 978-1-966253-00-6 (paperback)
ISBN 978-1-966253-02-0 (ebook)

Library of Congress Control Number: 2024926062

matchfactoryeditions.com

Book layout by RD Morgan

Cover art and design by Gretchen Hasse

Colophon design by Randy Cochran

*I dedicate this book to the memory
of Joseph Adam Henry Baeza (2002 – 2018).*

Table of Contents

Goodbye, 20th Century

Chicago is a poem with lines that break when there's no more land. I read it on foot, on my bike, on the CTA, and while I hang around, staring at buildings and the urban wildlife, decoding human faces, and cataloguing it all. Reinforced concrete crumbles, and engineers, taggers, street artists and I try our best to preserve it.

I live in this settler colony, in a settlement that became a metropolis in the previous century, in a building the same age as me. Memories of Yugoslavia and Europe have faded in my mind. They've moved into my molecules like a chronic viral infection. I perform lab tests on myself over and over with language as my only instrument.

i.

6:06 pm

Cars obedient in their owners' parking spots.
Staccato barks shatter my block's silence.
In my chest cavity—the old country.
On the outskirts of its towns,
apartments, shops, and factories
rub shoulders with sugar
beet and rapeseed fields. Organic
and synthetic matter burn together
there, and evening lights bring out
the youth, yards of denim,
the elderly in wool layers,
chestnuts in their char-covered hands.
Tossed newspaper cones unfurl
in the wind and the drizzle. I can read the ink
of our cracking sphere, the old and the new,
the first, the second, and the third world,
Octobers and Novembers
of the past two hundred years.

Poets in Translation

This is a poem about poetry,
a tapestry of fragments,
a dialogue at a crowded party
with not enough dancing.

S sounds, snakes with artichokes.
L sounds, apples with butterflies.
M sounds, praying mantises with gummies.

What do they sing?

And who can hear, whose ears?

I fell from the train.
Did the agents storm the train
at a stop in a village by the border?
Did the provincial agents
search everyone's stuff?
Did folks panic and throw
papers out the window?
Do all documents contain secret words?
Are all the living, breathing
bodies hidden
to be smuggled across?

Everything became something
everything turned into shit.
All eternity: nothing!
I am beautiful but doomed
if sound and meaning

matter more than the labor
of fingers around pencils
fingertips on keys
moving in a trance.

The poet knows how to remember
all the paradoxes and the grasping.

The border line was
end-stopped, once. Now,
it would break
through the margins.

This is my science of care—
my being and the other being
man-machine and poetry-science,
and poets always worry
about beauty and botany and fire.

Youbeyondmy

You are a Yugoslavia beyond my mind's eye
—Harryette Mullen, "Any Lit"

My opera has
Budget for no orchestra

My experiment is untranslatable
Youbeyondmy
A country no more
No less
My ex

My tongue saysings
What I mean to saysing
The way I mean
To saysing
The page
That's my tongue
My to

Too Many Memories in Tatters

Beaches marked with "No Swimming" signs. A weathered skeleton of an abandoned water park. A mound of dirt that pretends to be a ski slope. One day, my washing machine floods the kitchen, I place bath towels down to soak the water up, run to the porch not remembering the English idiom for   . It takes a long time. Language may be clay.

Spring Soup

I grew up and made dinner.
My spring soup is powder
and noodles, instructions printed
on the back of the bag.
I serve it to myself
in a bowl-and-spoon set
I purchased online, porcelain
or ceramic, I'm no longer sure.

In 1999, I could walk
to work or take the tram,
marginal alt-text in the code
of Prague. As one state crumbled,
another secret was erected,
all glory to cranes, cement, bulldozers.

Five Days of Reading Turkish Coffee Grounds

A flamenco dancer at the center, and she's creating a world, it seems. Turtles, foxes, snails, people, and a network of roots and growth.

A turtle (with a very long neck) about to climb up a living, erupting volcano. Or a snail with a very large shell, in the shadow of a mushroom cloud.

The flamenco dancer again. A bust of Karl Marx in the background. This time she's topless and masked: a white fox head and a pineapple crown.

A herd of horses atop a mountain in China. Horses, a plow, and a mound of dirt. A big comet in the sky above them. Behind them a blacksmith. Sparks fly.

A map of Eurasia, and three silhouettes: a girl child playing with a baby and a woman with two mounds of fleece she's about to spin into yarn.

Fable

The fox lives
in the abandoned
dormitory near the small
aircraft landing. The fox drinks
filtered Danube water and takes
walks in the workers' park
to the World War Two
monument at the center,
a concrete obelisk
graffitied on the bottom,
topped with an iron star.
The fox's fur is deep red too.
The fox drives the snowplow,
clears the path
for the neighborhood wildlife.

ii.

Parallel Lines

No lift. No mountain slopes.
No pairs of parallel lines. Even in the 80s

skiing was for the well-to-do. I'd stop
by a K67 for a hot dog and tea,

just a kid and a tough red plastic kiosk,
a bite, a sip, fogged up glasses.

Now it's hot pretzels after work, and work
never ends, but tap water remains

clear and odorless. I sing praises to chlorine
as it evaporates like a ghost of science.

One day workers ski resorts will reopen.
I'll find myself on a hilltop. I'll fall

and slide softly to the bottom on my back,
my skis a victory sign in the air,

for water processing plants,
for the well-to-do.

The Unemployed of the World

I apply the rest of my cologne,
step out to the balcony
to smoke. My world
is mid-century facades
designed in positivist offices
by architects and city planners
in checkered suits,
poring over blueprints
through thick lenses
in Michael Caine frames.
My world is concrete
that looks better
disfigured and stained,
my world is stray dogs,
garages and storage units,
bare poplars and maples.
Did the planners know
back in the 50s how we'd intervene
in their design with our desires, retinas,
and glitchy nervous systems?
We worked and lost our jobs.
I sit on my parquet floor
and arrange boxes of tea
in a semicircle around me.
I'll brew and brew all day, think of
domesticating a magpie.

Empire

There are life forms who slash the cheek
of a refugee, lay eggs like lizards, drown in their siestas.
Immigrants talk about papers, Dubai, Cambodia,
Singapore, migrate pleasure and work.
There was that "before," and now is that "after."
The loom industry minds the middle.

1992

As an undergrad, I fed my hunger
almost nothing. A cup of green Russian
tea at the Belgrade Philharmonic
Orchestra club served in a demitasse,
on a small plate with a sugar packet
and a silver spoon that had lost its sheen.
Undergrads and orchestra members sat
at parallel tables with glass ashtrays
and you lived with tobacco smoke
and ashes whether or not you indulged.

I fed the single bookshelf in my rented
apartment with soft- and hard-bound volumes,
two rows per shelf, many books acquired
through theft. Was I a talented thief or
did bookstores and libraries let me walk
away with the loot? The world had collapsed
by then. I fed my Walkman batteries.

I fed my hunger corn I would pop in a large
pot on the stove top. Sometimes an egg
stolen from an almost-empty supermarket.
I'd pretend I wanted to buy a quarter
of a loaf of day-old bread. They'd give it
to me for free. The salesclerk in her blue
uniform would pretend she did not know
there was an egg in the depths of my
coat pocket. The faint warmth of my thigh was
sending new information through the egg
shell to the very center of the yolk.

Imagine yourself

the Gulf Stream in August. And sink.
You think you're a secret, but it has never been you.

You will always be surrounded by lucky logograms.
Translate: Small dish.

Videos of all your memories will appear online.

The Next Noir

Instincts, I say, instincts:
dominoes toppling in the DNA spiral.

Whose covetous fingers
what ghost tore me apart
like a placard confiscated at a rally?
I'm learning how (muscles
contract when danger fills the air)
to fight back.

In the next noir
I'll show off my new skills
blocking even the most devious
enemies who speak
in saccharine registers
to soften me pussycat-like.

To learn how not to repeat
my last mission that
wound up in the abyss:
I jumped from the aircraft
and—nothing!
Parachute all tangled on my back
a bundle of silk
refusing to obey
the yank of my hand.

iii.

Touhy

I walk on a diagonal
from Clark to Paulina
snow and gravel
under the soles
of my black sneakers
oranges, apples, cabbage
in a sack slung
over my shoulder

we live in a building
made of cinderblocks
with a façade
of ochre brick
full of cracks

Touhy was a real
estate developer but
in Czech "touhy" means
"desires, longings"

at home I lie down
and feel my muscles relax
around these bones
under this skin
who am I to resist sleep
when I have nowhere to go
no one else to feed

every day I walk
on the Pratt pier

and watch the downtown
skyline cleave itself
into the fog
and the water

in Touhy Park
all that space
where kids play
soccer and softball
in warmer months
on expansive turf
now covered with snow
the first two tents side by side
a tiny new community

my body an acid factory
filled with desire:
to piss
on the machinery
of capital

July 2, 2019

In this city the shape of a butcher's knife,
neighbors still share laundry rooms,
cyclists stay in marked lanes. I know

about detention centers. I get ice cream
and a can of apricot-flavored agua con gas
for the march where we chant
and strike, but not all
the time, not all of us.

Later, I walk to the lake
at sunset. A ragged rainbow
above the skyline to the south,
a sole lightning bolt on the horizon.
Lifeguards are gone,
only red flags sit at their posts.

There are armored vehicles
on the streets of the capital
and last Saturday's rat
gasped for air in the alley,
but it was too late for her.
Monarchs on my block are
greatgrandchildren of larvae
that metamorphized

in Michoacán in early spring.
Who knows how
long this city would last.

I am an elevator

attached
to a brutalist

construction—
I see
city blocks
that fall

asleep amid
prickly weeds

I see a skein
of geese that land
on the surface

of the lake
like it's their job
to surprise on demand

Translation Manual

i.

Xenos cactus grows in no man's land between   and   . Juices are inviting, but I've forgotten the propaganda: dangerously potent or potentially dangerous? Umbrellas are €5 and their shadows tell time, black on white; alienation is a bit more costly. I squint, zoom in: billions of small waves, each little crest a miniscule supernova exploding against the pebbles and rocks. Life has its own riot under the surface.

ii.

Bodies cling together in spite of malice. The army creeps in the valley; city boulevards already shudder. We created our own history, an orphanage of runaway circus freaks in an art nouveau building with no running water. Artists, new or old, don't always think of practicality or collateral damage. It's murder, I told you I was doomed, only a temporary solution. The top cat, safe and helmeted, contemplates his next meal. Do I slip out with my guitar? Smuggle machine guns to the guerilla fighters out in the woods? Our appetite stronger than survival instinct, you hold my head under it, like they taught you in the spy program, like any disillusioned alley kid would. It's my turn to fetch the water. I've always known I would make a hell of a refugee.

Crow Coffee

A crow brews me coffee and my nose
delights, but my tongue wonders: poison?
I peel a tangerine, and now there's bergamot
on my fingers, under my nails, and the debris looks
part orange crystal, part white membrane.

My tongue cares only for the juice that hits
the roof of my mouth, the back of my throat,
but I remember
it's war, it's always been.
Just next door there's

barbed wire, and guards, and a camp.
I throw myself a bacchanal,
think of the prisoners and do nothing.
Here we all are in the Earth's atmosphere,
and outside the breathable zone there's nothing
everything, nothing.

Keep Moving

turn the corner
where yuppies and bums
spit without thinking
churn out worlds built atop
the 21st century mess
in Chicago, elsewhere too,
you've been elsewhere your youth

you've seen both sides of a moldy wall,
pushed open a jammed sliding door,
vandalized a "no trespassing" sign,
lost a six-headed police officer
in a manhole

Mornings

I'm a customer from the past
on the el platform at 9:15 am.
Kudzu vines creep up
looted old mansions.
It doesn't bother me
that the train runs
express all the way
to Divison while I
shiver on the South Side.
I laugh with the sun,
my fusion machine
that mints the gold
for future reparations.

What Did You Write on 3/24/20 in Chicago?

I wrote oatmeal in the morning, rolled oats, raspberries, and raw hemp seed. I wrote a cup of loose-leaf black tea imported from Russia while my oatmeal bowl cooled, Royal Tea Czar Nicolas II, the box said, the same emperor who ordered pogroms (the box omitted that part). His empire fell one March day, but people never learn. I wrote my red bowl, my rose-colored cereal, my maple syrup that glimmered over it all.

Exactly twenty-one years ago I spent that March day in Belgrade waiting for the missiles. The missiles arrived, and I went to my building's basement full of neighbors and books, an old Cadillac covered in dust, and no washers or dryers.

Today I wrote a hot shower at 10pm after I wrote the thermostat down to sixty-five. I wrote a hearty pasta dinner, a sauce I built on a foundation of celery, carrots, scallions, garlic, and red wine. I wrote two loads of laundry, four quarters per load in my building's basement, four quarters per load in the dryer. Had to revise the dryer cycle, my stuff still damp the first time, four quarters more. I wrote a hot shower in the afternoon, that's when my hair went from oily to clean under my fingers massaging my scalp. I wrote my body dry with my red towel, I wrote my skin supple with perfumed lotion.

In the progress of the pandemic I lived like a king—not because I deserved it—as petite bourgeoisie do before each collapse.

At the Washington stop

choose the stairs
over the escalator.
On the fourth step, a chicken

bone. Remember
last night's dream about climbing
up a wire fence to escape

the quickly rising ocean tide.
On the platform, skip over
stagnant urine. It seems

everyone shivers
for a different reason.
A police officer walks

her muzzled shepherd dog
in an engineered and broken world.
In our illness, we are animals
ill-equipped for life.

iv.

June 10, 2020

if what you want is jobs
for everyone, you are still the enemy,
you have not thought thru, clearly
what that means

     —Diane di Prima, "Revolutionary Letter #19"

outside my ground floor window
the sky turns darker than asphalt at 9am
as remnants of the storm disintegrate
soaking the concrete that looks better
disfigured and stained

I made my bed and now
I'm eating watermelon chunks on it
waiting for thunderstorms and gale winds
and a new pair of canvas lace-up shoes

once poets wanted to bring their spoken word to the people—
no one but other poets listened
and tourists came to gawk at the freaks

no more improvised
stages and microphones for me
no over-the-top delivery

maybe I'll fry some eggs
make some coffee
in that red enamel džezva made in Slovenia
we have sliced whole grain Italian bread
and the chickens live on an Amish or Mennonite farm
and I would like my words to live in silence

on a page or a screen in poor people's hands when
a break is needed
a break between two ambulances
two marches
a page to wait
till they get out of jail

Diane di Prima said, "Ask for anything"
and once again some us do
and the best protest poetry is composed
by victims in front of their murderers
in front of accomplices
in front of witnesses

this is not a protest poem
this is not a revolutionary letter
I have no advice for this campaign
except the echo of that one line
ASK FOR EVERYTHING

the rich are the only guilty ones
and the planet will be fine
without us

One

A monster, a blank
cipher, I resist
a small god of broken
and fused languages, revolve
on my red stage.
I'm an instrument strung with
rage and theft. My dress is crude
oil spilling down the stairs.

A Very Important Milkmaid

Among the comrades of our beloved Blue Line,
I remain upright, legs slightly apart, back straight,
chest open, chin up, gaze straight ahead,
a very important milkmaid, milking
every particle I can add to my stature. All over

Chicago, our engineered seagull habitat, soles
of my shoes stick to the tectonic plates
of the industrial era. Cement and steel
and concealed bolts keep all this together,
support my secret mission. It's only at

night when I'm at home, in my bed,
that I become no-one, a body. A set
of eyes, a gaze that sweeps and reaps alphabets
off of pages and screens and into my ever-
repairing and ever-deteriorating cells. A set

of ears, a listening that picks up the polyphonic
neighborhood behind the open window. A distant
siren. Midnight road vehicles. Intermodal rail traffic,
weighted down with ore and waste. Dogday cicadas
relax their abdomens, one timbal at a time.

Howard Street

Today Howard Street tried to throw up a smoke screen
as a warm April afternoon prepared for its stint
as a cold May night. As a child
I learned that sidewalks have concealed buttons
and I could kick each one loose, peel back the pavement,
reveal an old portage and a spool of twine caked in mud.

CTA Paulina & Howard Terminal

The "i" in Paulina is a diphthong. I mouth it. The "ow" in Howard, ditto. Wild violets, more diphthongs. A lady runs to catch bus #147—from here, it will hit Sheridan, and at Foster turn onto Lake Shore Drive. She might see the sky, the lake, harbors, lagoons, if she rides all the way. All our bodies pursue basic needs: a spot on an empty bus, two rolls of quarters, a day's work. When you pass by a small Rogers Park lawn, learn this: "The purple flowers may be sterile. The plain, unopened ones that shelter beneath leaves are not only fertile, but self-fertilizing." At the mall, a masked hero has just mopped the floors, and now she's vacuuming the rugs by the entrance. My nose remembers the sterilizing agent in a bucket—nameless, brandless, never advertised—from my janitor summer. I push the door with my arm. No eye contact, my glasses are pitch black, no greeting this time. "Thick clumps of rhizomes store water, survive, and send forth new shoots."

The Fargo Beach Report

It stormed today and hail gathered
on concrete balconies
from the late sixties. In the early seventies,
our elevator got that distinct smell:
organic matter, burned plastic,
tobacco, waste, the mechanism of ropes,
steel, and industrial lubricants.

The architect ached for construction workers
to build her a livable monument
that could grow into a hybrid organism,
an endless cycle of rebirth. She could use only reinforced
concrete that looks better disfigured and stained,
that will meet its end as a small planet of rubble
not too long after the architect's death.

It's April 2020 at the end of a cul-de-sac
where a young lady sees me and vanishes
in her vestibule. My glasses are foggy.
I face the lake alone, take off my mask,
my vision clears. The water olive green,
the ducks and the seagull are at ease.
The lake has reclaimed Fargo Beach.

Rock Statues

money buys sand
for man-made beaches
the lake laps up

the Park Department
buys riprap
to fight the lake

neighbors balance
pieces of rubble
on the riprapped beach
a smaller rock supports
the bigger
one

storms topple
rock statues
into the waves
the lake spits back
ice

Skokie Swift

on a suburban train painted yellow
I fill my lungs with the off-gas

                        molecules promise a
poppy field

and off we go
past forget-me-nots by the river

                     a desire to jump in and
float

             the train smells of burnt rubber
and then
             we all do

Jefferson Park Transit Center

Don't ask if thoroughfares
can take you to the center.
The center too is the periphery
and a promise. Time

can stretch around here,
advertise a store that makes wrist watches
an option. Dehydrated (possibly), a young man

just bounced into the present tense. And
look, his tattoo says just: Name.
I'll see you, Octavio,
when all languages fuse into
One Word.

Between

Mulberry is the only food silkworms will eat, all their carbs, fiber, protein and fat in clumps of sweet flesh each summer.

Plump flies land on the pale field of my shins in the shade of a crab-apple tree and four cops on bicycles. Children

emerge from the water speaking Italian. A single familiar word—asciugaman—a visible sound wave, our connection.

No lifeguards. Today I gleam in my orange top. I fight boredom. No rip currents.

A Span of Sand, Glass

Orange trash
cans can barely cling
to the asphalt beneath.
Diagonal avenues
can be erased and redrawn,
people move elsewhere.
The Grand Avenue Bridge spreads
its iron limbs high up in the air.
A barge lugs through.
What's inside
its tall yellow containers?
Coal. Lumber. The past
and future tense.

Laid Off, Laid Back

Night

9 pm: rust-dulled can opener
index finger knuckle bean-can cut

9:01:   spilled beans, spilled blood,
skin turns red, sink turns red

if time accelerates/decelerates without my knowledge

11 pm: let the bar smoke stink me up

11:02:   band aid dampened with beer

if there is a turbine in my left lung, smell of ash as I exhale

Morning

3 am: sleep spins on
the occupied territory
of a merry-go-round

3:13:   bar-smoke-soaked clothes
stink up my bedroom

if the radiator at birth is a sleek piece
of heavy industry, but then grows
a patina of wear&tear with corners
of corrosion, and finally I learn

to appreciate its unreliable warmth
radiating daily dust

6 am: band-aid-wrapped skin wrinkled and gray

Afternoon

1 2 pm: open the window

12:01:   snowflakes on the rusty window bars; I run
my fingers along, blood pulses,
cut knuckle enjoys the cold

12:10:   thicken the kitchen
air again
with red and black pepper

if a time of scarcity comes again, monthly united
nations rations with no dish detergent, just bars
of brown scentless soap, and every once in a while
there is a package from the government, still no
dish detergent, but packets of tang to wash down
peanut butter crackers

1 pm: leftover beans for lunch
my protein trampoline

Marginal Era

I ride a bicycle
along the margin of error. My October all

in shambles, cigarette filters
stick to my wheels. I used to be

poor and famous. I write letters to felons
to keep in touch with the inside world. When it rains,

I take the pink line downtown, sometimes fall
half-asleep. Half of my face turns to wax.

Sometimes I's the needle—the turntable
of the Loop spins the drowsy city.

v.

Orbison

Researchers have baked a loaf of bread with ancient Egyptian sourdough they extracted from a terracotta bowl fragment. They ate that loaf. People have always believed in the eternal return, etched that belief into pottery, slid choruses into songs, inserted steel rods into cinder blocks. They knew. Concrete is more beautiful disfigured and stained. Roy Orbison once released a song without a chorus, a different chord progression for each verse. He sang with his whole vocal range. The phrase "in dreams" returned again and again. Radio DJs played the song, it was February '63. Those radio waves carried Roy into deep space at the speed of light. It's 2020. Roy has reached the system of Mu Arae and its planets. Visible from the southern hemisphere. Researchers have detected a rocky planet there that makes a full circle around its sun in ten Earth days. Write on an empty stomach before sleep. Or don't. Everything. Is all right.

Columns

In the city of Guanajuato
a folk artist remains outside the frame
of a PBS travel show.

Students walk up the stairs
of the old monastery.
They are columns that built themselves

out of mud left over
after they drained the river
for the system of silver mines.

Now they plot a sabotage action,
unwritten, undrawn.
A comic book!

Monk's Mood

Monk left North Carolina on a Greyhound bus.
I packed him a dissonance sandwich
and a thermos of black keys.

Early Cinema

When circuses pitched their tents
near aspen-lined roads in the provinces,
a dangerous woman imagined
streetcars she could ride unaccompanied,
and in her fantasy streetcars stood
for something else, something red.
First film crews parked their equipment
just down the road
and got all the footage of dying folk
customs they needed. They shot the woman
being crowned the queen of her town's carnival.
She would trade her headpiece made of foliage
for the world of cabarets, industrial pollution, steam.
Headpieces stood for something else,
something

From Stein to Smith

Lifting belly is so kind.
This bridge cannot end as it ends
where the prison's poplar swings
veined by the spoors of homesickness.

The low harm art
trembles in my shoe
in cathedral, museum, cloister,
at wood tables in factories.

Brilliant function of the land's disease,
I am a lagoon woman
bound for Black Mountain:
me, my razor, and my gun.

Fish and kelp

in a steaming bowl
wait on the counter.
I pay and take
my seat by the door.
A man must face
power but with
a spoon in his hand
and a white napkin
under his chin.

Power

A delivery drone.
A child-rearing cyborg.
A NASA robot that services the aging
satellites in our orbit.

A lionfish-hunting machine transported
by unmanned boats to Bermuda.

I am your new pet: moisture-responsive,
electronic, I crawl with no external
power source.

Sisters

I

Our childhood is fuzzy yellow,
their adulthood regulation blue.
We act quiet in bright polyester,
pretend cicadas could deafen us.

The rusty iron gate opens
and we take our positions
at the park's tennis court,
but you want to build a harbor,
reverse a river,
drain a lake,
pen a manifesto,
kick the solar rock.

II

My clothes fit you and you too ride a purple bike.
We compete on the tennis court that glows at night and

makes living trophies of us both. You admire
my subterranean loneliness. You're always about to

hit the ball, and then your arms drop, fatigued
from the laughter that sustains us. I look up

to you although you grow invisible
as lights dim. I know myself well.

III

I have a violet
bruise, petal-shaped,
on the inside
of my left arm

I imagine blood
rushing in defense
I don't remember
what happened

a tennis ball
my racket missed
or the handle
of my bike

a punch of the oversized
button on my new dress
with three-quarter sleeves
showing off my bracelets

our coach says our tools are not just extensions
of our hands wrists forceps
biceps shoulders
with our tools we are whole

vi.

My Anthropocene

I am a lowercase me in the chilly breeze
strung out folks wait wait wait
I walk in my ballet flats,
pencil skirt, boatneck sweater

stop at the green light
why won't she go
why this instant
tension at the x

sprinkle my inquiry
shake the space station
pet Mayakovsky's cat
under the traffic light
that only shows
three phases of the moon

I will live your futurism
If you will live mine

I see wet cement and imagine
softly imprinting my naked
back in that porridge of silicates and oxides
one vertebra at a time

that's how I'll leave
my fossil trace no paleontologist
will ever need

Calendulas

All the pristine black vehicles are the low notes
in this film score, with their tinted windows,
and the passengers' moving desire for safety.
All the cups in panhandlers' hands
are full of calendulas. The lake and the prairie

birth a fog machine for the special effects
that flatten all the hotels, all the glass shopping centers,
for the high drama of softened features high up
among window washers. Lavanderia carts arrive,
filled with volumes of old narratives and poems.

My fingers turn yellow against the cloth-bound
covers, gilded spines, generous print, pages
never read. The smell of ink and cellulose,
once trapped for the future, is released like
a good ghost. The former regime, in the long-gone

state, ended with the people singing the only
folk song they knew, the one recorded on cassettes
and broadcast via radio waves ad nausea.
That signal has long passed the first frog star.
Under the new regime, fears drown in the sound

of seagulls, cicadas, horses, squirrels, and dogs.
We can't wait to be drowned out.
We crack open our aluminum cans. Our drinks fizzle.
If you take a sip, a gulp, and a mouthful, the invisible
hand strikes a chord.

Plowman

Never forgive your
masters and never

place grains on my plate: augurs are
eating lunch with me today. We're arguing
passionately, I'm letting my plum

be a plum. See how its flesh shines,
skating over my tongue's
edge. Bread crusts will

never rot. I promise to always
run out of time, cut that
corner, cultivate
life at this creamery, grow a chestnut
tree in the middle of the line. The cook

turns the spit. Plowman,
plowman, thank you, now
splash some water on your overheated engine,
sun your arms and
legs. Your limbs remember the
ship that delivered your first tractor.

The sky
is a blueberry in your mouth.

Engineered Verse

Who else, in doorways and viaduct shelters, dreams of
the last two cities they liked? Don't ask. They fuck and sleep

by the lakeshore and in prairie gardens. Less than a beast,
Chicago is a cell under the cosmic microscope lens

focused on the swamp underneath, not the industry people
with promises all gritty on their tongues,

it's hunger, green appetite and soil desire,
not my metallic blue-gray need. Steam rises from the sand

and up to the windows stacked above the concrete
that looks better disfigured and stained.

I read train tracks along urban rivers,
couplets of engineered verse, sleek wilderness.

Didn't bring a coat when I migrated to this colony named
Chicago. Borrowed all the money. Never earned my keep.

Acceptance Speech

I'd like to thank two Rogers Park mansions
where nobody lives. The Emil Bach house and
the Lang house landscapers, receptionists,
carpenters, janitors, electricians,
painters, security guards who work there,
thank you, tourists and wedding parties,
thank you. Caterer who spilled
some mixed berry compote
on the bride's gown, thank you.
I'd like to thank the security camera
for capturing a good angle of my face.
Thank you for inducting me into
the Loitering Hall of Fame.
I'd like thank Dorothea Lange and my team
of well-fed cats, thank you for the honor.
I've only just begun.

The Poet Is in the House (an Afterword)

I. Some General Ideas Behind This Book

So you've been assigned this book by a teacher or a book club? You are maybe wondering what the poet meant to say? Reader, I'll try to help.

The title of the book appears verbatim or slightly paraphrased in several poems (go count them!) in the book. As you read the book, you move together with the narrator through urban landscapes, the narrator who is haunted by the feeling that today's world is a future archeological site. Today's world is collapsing, and these lines and sentences are a record, a testimony kept for someone far in the future. But the book is not all doom and gloom. There is flora and fauna, flights of fancy, food, and other fun "f" words.

What about rhyme? There's no rhyme in the poems in this book, and some poems eschew line breaks altogether! Reader, this is deliberate. I can and do write rhymed poetry. But because I'm a musician as well as a poet, my rhymed verse exists in the form of my songs, and everything else ends up in the form of printed and (when I read it aloud) spoken word.

Doom and gloom vs. fun and games is not the only way in which the book is bringing together two opposites. It's also in the lyric-anti-lyric push-and-pull in my work in general. On the one hand, this book is pretty traditional: the narrator has this distinct, individual lyric voice created by Snežana Žabić (b. 1974), even though the poems are not always autobiographical, and often they are completely fictional or even fantastical.

On the other hand, the book is deliberately pushing against the lyric tradition by employing procedural experiments to generate textual collages seemingly out of thin air, out of the raw material of language and free associations as opposed to lived experience and logical thought.

The first poem in the book, "Goodbye, 20th Century" is pretty explicit and clear. This, reader, is also deliberate. For those who read the book cover to cover, the opening poem is a key to understanding what the book will deliver: Chicago, Yugoslavia, Europe, language, this moment in time, and references that go deep into the 20th century.

The rest of the poems are grouped into six sections. "6:06pm" opens the first section of the book, and it's the first one explicitly about Europe, "the old country", with images summoned from my childhood memories of my hometown, the rest of Yugoslavia, and other countries I lived in or visited. It was 6:06pm when I sat down to write the first draft of the poem, which I thought was a significant coincidence because 606 is the beginning of the 5-digit postal code of every neighborhood in Chicago, IL.

Yugoslavia happens to be where I'm from, and that country fell apart in 1991. During its final three decades, Yugoslavia was a socialist country with capitalist elements, rather open borders, and an international outlook as a founding member of the nonaligned movement, a buffer zone between the Cold-War-embroiled East and West.

Before it failed, Yugoslavia succeeded, and I think all of us who want to believe that another world is possible should remember that. Another world happened once, in a small place, and so another world might be built again, somewhere, at some point, a more humane alternative to what we're living now. Another world, or "Yugoslavia beyond my mind's eye," as Harryette Mullen writes in her poem "Any Lit" in her book *Sleeping with the Dictionary*, referenced in my poem "Youbeyondmy." Mullen's poem "Any Lit" is a litany (get it?) of her improvisations on the African American folk courtship wordplay "you are a... beyond my..." and Yugoslavia appeared in her poem on the basis of sound, (you-Yu), not an ideological agenda.

Sometimes my poems intentionally don't mention any geographical locations or years, and sometimes they do, but my intent is often to combine, in a single poem or a single sentence, images that refer to things I experienced on both sides of the pond in both the 20th and the 21st century. My poems are small, often-malfunctioning, time-traveling aircraft that transport you back and forth between worlds until you're as exhausted and disoriented as any immigrant. You don't have to be an immigrant to read this book, though it might help if you are.

Some poems are results of procedures, and "Five Days of Reading Turkish Coffee Grounds" is a case in point. Around the world, people (often those whose ancestors lived in or very close to the Ottoman Empire) brew and drink unfiltered coffee, which leaves a layer of soggy brown coffee grounds on the bottom of their white cups. When they gather with friends and family to socialize over coffee, they'll often stare at their dirty emptied cups until their minds recognize images in those coffee grounds. Then they interpret those images and predict each other's future. Some even believe that there's something to that game, if not prophetic, then maybe something therapeutic?

I've "told future" to friends, just making crap up and shaping it into vague predictions or veiled advice. So, one day I decided to drink a cup of Turkish coffee and write a few lines based on what my brain discerns in my dirty emptied cup. The next day I did that again. The next day, ditto. The fourth day, I thought, this could go on, a poem that would keep growing day by day, to be finished only when my body with a mind is finished living. But it only went on for five days. On the sixth day, I stared at my cup and saw nothing but soggy brown grounds on the bottom of my white cup, and that meant my poem was finished.

Another procedural poem is "Plowman." It started with W. H. Auden's famous poem "Musée des Beaux Arts," from December 1938, that reflects on the human condition via a famous Brueghel's painting of the death of Icarus.

W. H. Auden is not one of my favorite poets, and "Musée des Beaux Arts" is not one of my favorite poems. But when I teach forms of poetry, and I want to show students examples of famous ekphrastic poems (poems that reference, describe, or reflect on pieces of visual art), we look at the digital copy of the Breughel painting projected on the big classroom screen, and we read that poem.

One day I was preparing to teach, and I decided to pluck a word from somewhere inside each line of "Musée des Beaux Arts" except the last one, and I picked: never, masters, place, eating, passionately, be, skating, edge, never, run, corner, life, tree, turns, ploughman, splash, sun, legs, ship, the sky. I don't remember why I took nothing from the last line. I just know I wrote the words I picked down as a list and continued creating my lines, playfully improvising until I had my fill.

Both my more lyric and my more experimental, procedural poems, are rooted in my attitude about poetry: when poetry gets pompous, when a poet takes themselves too seriously, I'm turned off. I don't take my poetry too seriously, yet on the other hand, I work hard on it. And while working hard on it, I'm always conscious that to write poetry is to play, to experience pleasure and to provide pleasure. That's kind of anti-lyric if you think about it, given that traditional lyric poetry is aiming to provide something much more pretentious, even pompous, like deep epiphanies or universal truths, and the like.

II. Questions and Answers

Danica Pavlović, a great poet from Belgrade, Serbia, wonders about the English language. "You sound like you don't have our accent when you speak or read aloud in English. Is that how you speak now, in Chicago English?"

I love that question because not a single native speaker of Chicago English would be deaf to my (albeit slight) foreign accent. Chicagoans' guesses about my accent have ranged from Baltic to Scandinavian to Middle Eastern to Latin American (and specific countries within those regions) and of course Russian. Whichever guess they offer, I compliment them: "That's a good guess!"

Danica's question made me wonder perhaps for the first time why I speak with a *slight* Serbo-Croatian accent, while, for example, Marina Abramović seemingly cultivates a *strong* Serbo-Croatian accent. I strive to be understood when I speak, and I worry that a thicker accent would impede that. But I have to admit: I probably don't want to be immediately identified as a foreigner and especially not a Balkan/Yugoslav immigrant. I'm not proud of that. I'm not ashamed either.

There's no doubt that the way we speak is an outpouring of our identity, but our identity is a slippery animal. And as much as I'm a walking museum of late-20th-

century Yugoslavia and Europe, to me that's just the cards I was dealt, excuse the mixed metaphor. Another card I was dealt was 21st-century Chicago. I'm playing the card game, but I'm no gambling addict.

Danica also wants to know about my concept for the book, which is: I'm writing for someone in the future who will live on the other side of our current global collapse and will be interested in the testimonies of the people who lived in the 2020s or so. She points out a paradox between that intent of the book and the lines in "My Anthropocene": "that's how I'll leave / my fossil trace no paleontologist / will ever need." So what is it? Poetry as testimony for far-future readers or ephemeral scraps? I say, both, fully aware how absurd it all is.

Writing poetry means being ignored. Of course it will languish in obscurity and be buried under the rubble of video games and porno movies, to mention but two genres that are much more important to people.

But that poem "My Anthropocene" has something else in it that delights me and may delight you too. That outfit? "Ballet flats, pencil skirt, boatneck sweater"? I've never in my life worn it. I included them because I'm fascinated by terms for clothing items that function as compound nouns where the modifying noun is not referring to, say, the material from which the clothing item is made (e.g. "leather", "linen", "wool") but rather functions metonymically or metaphorically.

The poem also mentions Vladimir Mayakovsky (1893-1930). He was extremely famous when he was alive: people either wanted to be him or to be with him. And he is still being read. We read him to delight in his play with the Russian language or we read translations to delight in how the translator then plays in the target language trying to become Mayakovsky in a way. We read Mayakovsky in the original or in translation, and that's how we communicate with the past that's long gone but may return in some new form.

The past always has something to tell us about our present and about the future. Danica says: "Maybe poetry written today will indeed be more interesting in the future, to someone." But then, Ksenija Simić-Mueller, a great mathematician and poet from Tacoma, WA (originally from Belgrade), adds: "If anyone in the future will read anything at all."

It is also possible that there will be no literacy in the future. Danica agrees: "We don't know what will happen in the future." It's best to leave that topic behind and consider some down-to-earth practical matter.

To that end, Ksenija wanted to know: "What's with the six numbered sections in the book? How did you group the poems?"

That's a great question that allows me to say this: these lyric/anti-lyric poems I write are wild things that are begun one day, fully drafted another day, and then revised over varied periods of time. They don't form any kind of a narrative; nor do they want to be grouped thematically or chronologically. In this book, each of the six groups of poems let the themes of the book flow and melt into one another: language and its limits in the face of global and local cataclysms of various sorts, most of which began in the 20th century; Chicago as one of the smallest global metropolises; work; solidarity with fellow workers; refusal of the whole "eat the rich or die trying" attitude.

III.   Additional References

In the above section, I explained a few of the references I made in the book. But wait, there's more!

"Five Days of Reading Turkish Coffee Grounds" mentions Karl Marx. This was a 19th century philosopher who theorized with his friends and lovers about their own collapsing world, and he was the most prolific of the bunch by far.

"Fable" mentions a fox I saw in Borovo Naselje, Croatia, in December 2018. I was thinking of that fox when I was reading *Fox* by Dubravka Ugrešić, my favorite novelist.

"Parallel Lines" mentions K67, a type of a modular, fiberglass kiosk that was everywhere in Yugoslavia when I was growing up. A replica of it was exhibited in the MoMA exhibit *Toward a Concrete Utopia: Architecture in Yugoslavia 1948-1980*.

"The Unemployed of the World" mentions Michael Caine, a bespectacled 60s "swinging London" movie star, who made large black plastic frames cool while playing a spy on the big screen.

The wordplay of "migrate pleasure" in "Empire" comes from comically faulty close captioning that accompanied the opening remarks during a 2017 event in Chicago celebrating 100 years of Gwendolyn Brooks, a poet your teacher or book club will hopefully also assign.

"July 2, 2019" doesn't represent some historic date. There was a protest that day in Chicago expressing solidarity with immigrants terrorized by ICE. I know that the first line echoes a line by poet Orit Gidali (b. 1974), but I no longer remember which poem.

There were Black Lives Matter protests on "June 10, 2020" around the world, an outpouring of grief for victims of police violence and rage against the system that made that violence quotidian. An adjunct professor working remotely, I stayed in lockdown while people like my brother-in-law Mario Garcia, a Riverwalk security guard in downtown Chicago, had to physically go to work. Mario's way to express support for the protesters was to take pictures and videos and, as a citizen reporter, post them to social media. I was reading Diane di Prima (1934-2020), among other poets, a lot those days. But di Prima is one of my favorites.

"CTA Paulina & Howard Terminal" incorporates quotes from an article I found online, by Jackie Rhoades, "Killing Wild Violets – Tips for Wild Violet Control," slightly adapted.

"Jefferson Park Transit Center" mentions Octavio, and it isn't really Octavio Paz (1914-1998), a famous poet from Mexico. His poem "Fable" (translated by Eliot Weinberger) has these lines: "There was only one huge word with no back to it / A word like a sun / One day it broke into tiny pieces," but you should really read that whole poem and more by Paz, I think you'll like it.

Roy Orbison (1936-1988) was a Texas troubadour of the highest order.

Thelonious Monk (1916-1982) was a jazz musician born in Rocky Mount, NC. If you take a Greyhound bus on the route between Wilmington, NC, and Richmond, VA, as I had done many times 2002-2005, you'll see Rocky Mount, NC, and maybe you'll think of Thelonious Monk.

"From Stein to Smith" is composed of lines originally by the poets that are explicitly named in the poem that didn't make the cut when I put together *Concrete Is More Beautiful Disfigured and Stained*:

> Gertrude Stein bought a great many wax candles.
> Marina Tsvetayeva saved shadow money.
> Anna Akhmatova howled under the towers.
> Nelly Sachs collected the seed of the dandelion blossom.
>
> Emily Dickinson carried a loaded gun.
> Edith Södergran discovered her dimensions.
> H.D. was pleased with the straggling company of the brush.
> Diane di Prima cooked daisies in her soup.
>
> Muriel Rukeyser measured effects of friction: to fight.
> Maria Sabina went through the sea with an open book.
> Bessie Smith taught the birds to sing bass.

This outtake poem is also composed of lines originally written by those eleven poets. Both poems are therefore in the cento form: a patchwork of fragments written by others.

Dorothea Lange (1895-1965) appears in "Acceptance Speech." She was a photographer most famous for documenting American lives during the Great Depression.

IV.   A Parting Thought

I hope that helps. But if you're confused about anything, feel free to email me at sz@matchfactoryeditions.com.

If you are reading this after I'm dead, reader, I'm afraid I won't be able to get back to you.

Acknowledgements: The Work of Poetry

According to UNESCO, the youth literacy rate was 91% in 2016, while the adult literacy was 86% on a planet that numbers 7.5 billion. Out of those, hundreds of millions can read poetry in English.

I worked on this book as if hundreds of millions would read it. And I didn't work alone. I am grateful to spousal comrade Nicolas Garcia and friends who critiqued my manuscript: Jennie Berner, Tasha Fouts, Dubravka Juraga, Paul Martinez Pompa, Nadya Pittendrigh, and Dawn Tefft.

And without RD Morgan as my editor, the manuscript would not have become this book.

In solidarity, I also want to give a shoutout to my fellow contingent faculty and all my former and current students at The Chicago Academy for the Arts, Loyola University Chicago, The City Colleges of Chicago, University of Illinois at Chicago, University of North Carolina at Wilmington, University of Maryland Global Campus, and Southern New Hampshire University.

Some poems in this volume have previously appeared, sometimes in different versions, in lit journals and anthologies:

"Poets in Translation" and "The Unemployed of the World" in *Atlanta Review*

"Translation Manual" in *Coconut*

"I am an elevator" in *Scoundrel Times*

"From Stein to Smith" in *Blood Tree Literature*

"My Anthropocene," "Empire," "1992," "A Very Important Milkmaid," "Calendulas," and "Five Days of Reading Turkish Coffee Grounds" in *Apofenie*

"Power" and Monk's Mood" in *Vernacular*

"What Did you Write on 3/24/2020 in Chicago" in *And Then: Stories About What Happens Next*, Agitator Gallery, Chicago, 2020

"At the Washington stop" in *Jelly Bucket*

I am thankful to the editors.

Damir Šodan has translated the following poems into Serbo-Croatian for the journal *Poezija*: "Plowman," "Engineered Verse," "Acceptance Speech," Marginal Era," "Columns," Sisters," Power," "Orbison," and "Youbeyondmy." Hvala, Damire!

About the Author

Chicago-based transnational writer and musician Snežana Žabić is the author of the short story collection *U jednom životu* (KOS, Serbia, 1996), the hybrid memoir *Broken Records* (punctum books, USA, 2016), and the poetry collections *Po(jest)zija/Po(eat)ry* (SKC NS, Serbia, 2013) written with Ivana Percl, and *The Breath Capital* (New Meridian Arts, USA, 2016). Her work is included in *Cat Painters: An Anthology of Contemporary Serbian Poetry*, edited by Dubravka Đurić and Biljana Obradović (Lavender Ink/Diálogos Press, USA, 2016). She plays guitar, writes songs, and sings in Rent Party, everyone's favorite feminist garage folk band. She teaches writing and literature as a part of the contingent academic workforce and has been a proud union member of UIC GEO, SEIU Faculty Forward, and UIC United Faculty.

www.ingramcontent.com/pod-product-compliance
Lightning Source LLC
Chambersburg PA
CBHW051328120626
46547CB00015B/2447